Podcast Promotion and Growth with Social Media

Table of Contents

We don't have a choice on whether we DO social
media, the question is how well we DO it.

— Erik Qualman

Chapter 1. Introduction

Unleashing the power of social media for your podcast's phenomenal growth? Sounds like a stellar game plan! Welcome to our Special Report on Podcast Promotion and Growth with Social Media – a lively, insightful exploration to arm you with top-of-the-chart strategies. This report, brimming with hot tips and successful tactics, will be your faithful aide whether you're launching your first podcast or aiming to give an existing one a fresh boost. Remember, it's not about plugging in headphones and tuning into silent growth. It's about amplifying your voice, reaching millions, and creating an impact. So, pull up a chair, grab your favorite beverage and let's embark on this exciting journey together - boosting your podcast into its next orbit of success! Get ready to command the power of social media and let YOUR podcast roar loud and clear across platforms!

Chapter 2. Understanding the Podcast Landscape

The podcast universe undoubtedly resembles a vibrant constellation of ideas, voices, and perspectives spread across the digital realm. As entrancing as it might be, it can be equally overwhelming, especially when you're seeking to establish a distinctive presence in such a dynamic arena. With millions of podcasts and billions of podcast episodes, it's vital to understand the podcasting landscape before you architect your victory.

2.1. The Evolution of Podcasting

While podcasts first surfaced around 2004, it wasn't until around 2013 that they began to gain substantial traction. Early pioneers swept through limitations, truly democratizing the platform by permitting anyone with an engaging voice to have a shot in the limelight. Podcasts boomed due to the fusion of engaging narrative and the cell phone's growing prevalence, enabling listeners to consume information on-the-go.

Over time, podcasts evolved from a novelty into mainstream media with the potential to address a global audience. As of 2022, there are over two million podcasts and over 48 million podcast episodes globally, growing at an exponential rate. The global podcasting market size is predicted to reach USD 41.8 billion by 2026, with faster download and streaming speeds facilitated by 5G networks, proving the medium's potential for growth and the essentiality to understand its landscape.

2.2. Understanding the Audience

Regardless of your podcast's content, it will fail to fulfill its purpose if the target audience remains a mystery to you. Who are these dedicated podcast listeners? What kind of content do they desire? What devices do they use to consume the medium? The key to reaching your audience lies in comprehending these finer details.

Stats reveal that 68% of the U.S. population consists of podcast listeners. In terms of gender breakdown, 36% of male U.S. internet users listen to podcasts, and the same holds true for 29% of female users.

These listeners are mostly on the move, with 49% of podcast listening occurring at home and 22% while driving. Families and full-time employees form a sizeable proportion of the audience as they can conveniently integrate podcast listening into their daily chores or commute. To deliver a podcast that resonally truly with your listeners, understanding their routines, interests, and preferences is integral.

2.3. The Diversity of Podcast Genres

Podcasting is a flexible medium which allows it to accommodate practically any topic you can envisage, from politics and criminal justice to food, health, and fashion. A look at some podcasting platforms reveals that the most popular podcasting genres include news, comedy, society & culture, and sports.

Each genre attracts a specific kind of audience, which further calls for a careful assessment of the genre under which your podcast could best thrive. Considering the genre will help shape your content, direct your promotional efforts toward the right audience and increase the chances of your podcast's success.

2.4. The Power of Podcasting Platforms

Numerous podcasting platforms cater to your various publishing needs. These platforms, namely Apple Podcasts, Spotify, and Google Podcasts among others, not only host your podcasts but also promote your content, furnish detailed analytics, and handle revenue options if monetization is in your scheme. Each platform has varying user bases, showcasing different listener preferences. Identifying the optimal platform is crucial as it is pivotal in reaching your target audience effectively.

2.5. Setting Up Your Podcast for Successful Execution

Understanding the podcasting landscape is incomplete without setting up the right equipment and environment. A basic podcasting setup would require a good quality microphone, headphones, and some form of audio recording and editing software. However, the setup grows more intricate depending on your needs – interviewing guests, having co-hosts, recording in different locations, or live streaming.

Creating a comfortable and serene environment conducive to focusing and expressing your thoughts is as crucial as your technical equipment. Ensure a calm, soundproof space to record your podcast in order to avoid disturbances while recording.

2.6. Legalities in Podcasting

Key legal issues like copyright and defamation laws must not be overlooked. Podcasters ought to be wary of the underlying rules about using music or clips from copyrighted works, giving credence to other people's work, mentioning defamatory content concerning any person, etc. Staying aware and cautious of these legalities guarantees your podcast a trouble-free journey.

In this chapter, we have painted a comprehensive portrait of the podcasting landscape. With the above understanding, you are better equipped to venture into the world of podcasting with informed decisions and strategic flair. As we progress further into this report, we will unlock how you can leverage this understanding to effectively harness the power of social media for promoting your podcast and achieve resounding success.

Chapter 3. Essentials of Effective Podcasting

In the realm of podcasting, a series of crucial factors determine the success and impact of your output. Recognizing these essentials and implementing them effectively is key to creating a standout podcast that commands attention and fosters loyalty among listeners. In this exploration, we dive deep into these posers, understanding them in context and providing actionable strategies on how to best utilize these prerequisites for a resonating podcast venture.

3.1. Crafting a Distinctive Podcast Theme

The inception of any podcast begins with defining a compelling theme, one with which you possess both passion and expertise. This foundational element separates your podcast from the myriad of others, increasing visibility and attracting loyal listeners. The theme should resonate with a specific demographic, thereby accessing a niche audience invested in your subject matter. Keep in mind, however, that being overly specialized might limit your audience reach, whereas being overly general might not strike a chord with any particular group. Navigating through this fine balance is crucial to hitting that sweet spot.

3.2. Ensuring Exceptional Audio Quality

Practitioner skills aside, technicalities also play a significant role in any podcast's success. One such technicality, fundamental yet important, is audio quality. Amateurish sound quality can immediately deter listeners, painting an unprofessional image. Invest in a good microphone and audio editing software to ensure clear and crisp sound. Advanced technology such as noise-canceling headphones or studio soundproofing might be a worthwhile investment down the line. Moreover, learning basic skills in sound editing plays a vital role in achieving smooth and high-quality audio.

3.3. Engaging in Effective Scripting

While the charm of spontaneity attracts some listeners, effective scripting underpins a successful podcast. Scripting doesn't mean reading verbatim from a prepared text; instead, it entails having a thorough plan for each podcast episode. Lay out the key points you want to discuss, interesting anecdotes to share, and crucial questions for your prospective guests. An engaging script allows you to maintain your podcast's structure and flow, reducing the risk of aimless rambling or awkward silences.

3.4. Incorporating Engaging Podcast Formats

Different podcast formats resonate with different audience demographics. From solocasts and interviews to roundtable discussions and investigative storytelling, the format you choose can greatly influence the reception of your podcast. Incorporate a variety of formats to keep your content fresh and your audience engaged. Remember, however, that the choice of format should align with your podcast theme. Accordingly, select a medium that best supports your content and appeals to your target listeners.

3.5. Maintaining Consistent Podcast Release Schedule

Consistency is key in the realm of podcasting. Podcasting platforms favor podcasts that regularly release content, and regular episodes keep listeners coming back for more. Determine a release schedule that suits your resources and audience expectations. Whether bi-weekly or monthly – consistency trumps frequency. Plan and record episodes in advance to adhere to your schedule.

3.6. Engaging, and Responding to Listener interaction

Fostering a strong relationship with your audience will nurture your podcast community. Engage with your listeners via emails, comments, social media, or even dedicated podcast platforms. Allocate a part of your podcast for listener interaction, like addressing their questions or discussing their feedback. This enhances listener loyalty, making them feel valued and involved.

Incorporating these essentials paves the way to effective podcasting. Bear in mind, though, that there are no quick yields. Podcast growth requires patience, persistence, trials and corrections, but with the right blend of passion and diligence, podcast success is indeed within reach! In succeeding chapters, we bust the codes of leveraging social media for podcast growth, diving into specific platforms and strategies – a handy guide for your podcast's phenomenal growth. Stay tuned!

Chapter 4. Leveraging Social Media for Podcast Growth

As you step into the bustling realm of social media, it's essential to have a clear understanding of its immense potential and how it can be harnessed to scale your podcast audience.

4.1. Why Use Social Media for Podcast Promotion?

The power of social media lies in its broad reach and diverse user base. A variety of social media platforms offer a unique blend of demographics, enabling podcast creators to target a broad or very specific audience. Each platform serves as a potential channel to promote your podcast, build a committed listener base, and interact with your audience. Social media platforms can supplement your podcast by offering interactive content, updates, and discussion forums that can engage the audience beyond the auditory scope of the podcast.

Social media promotion is not just about publicizing episodes but about building a community around your podcast. It's about starting conversations, sparking debate, fostering fan engagement, and turning casual listeners into loyal followers.

4.2. The Power of Platform Selection

Before you open a dozen accounts on every social media network available, take a step back. Remember, it's not about being everywhere; it's about being where your potential listeners are. Every social media platform offers unique features and appeals to different demographics. Dig into the data, know who your audience is and where they socialize online. Choose platforms where you can leverage your podcast niche.

4.3. Break Down Barriers with Authenticity

In a world saturated with digital content, authenticity cuts through noise. Be original and genuine in your approach to social media. Authenticity fosters trust and loyalty, two critical factors that convert one-time listeners into habitual podcast followers. Share behind-the-scenes glimpses, involve your audience in the creative process, respond to comments and demonstrate that at the core of your podcast, there's a real person with passion and dedication.

4.4. Dive into Different Content Formats

Social media platforms offer a buffet of content formats, each with their unique appeal. Make use of images, videos, infographics, audiograms, and more to engage your audience. Remember, it's not always about promoting your latest episode; it's about providing value to your listeners. Post relevant, engaging content that amplifies your podcast's unique perspective and reflects your brand's voice. Diversify your content but maintain consistency in your messaging.

4.5. Strategy for Scheduling: Consistency is Key

The frequency of posting is not as crucial as consistently delivering quality content. Develop a posting schedule that works for you and stick to it. Consistency is a testament to your commitment and builds listener anticipation. Utilize scheduling tools to automate posts and ensure steady social media activity.

4.6. Engagement: The Heart of Your Social Media Strategy

Social media is not a one-way street. It's a dynamic, interactive space where engagement is king. Respond to comments, encourage discussion, and create opportunities for your audience to interact with you and each other. User-generated content and contests can boost audience involvement. Increasing engagement raises your visibility on social media algorithms, extending your reach.

4.7. Use Analytics to Drive Strategy

Data is your guiding light in the ocean of social media. Utilize platform-specific analytics to understand what works and what doesn't. Track engagement metrics, audience demographics, and peak activity times. Use this data to refine your strategy, hone your messaging, and maximize your impact.

In conclusion, leveraging social media for your podcast's growth must not be an afterthought. It requires strategic planning, consistent execution, and adaptability. Achieving podcast growth via social media is a long game that requires patience. But, with commitment and persistence, your podcast can harness this digital arena to reach new heights of listenership and engagement.

Chapter 5. Strategic Use of Facebook for Podcast Promotion

To propel your podcast's success to greater heights, one cannot overlook the strategic importance of Facebook - a digital powerhouse boasting billions of users globally. Like a bounty of ripe fruits hanging from a tree, this behemoth presents a fertile ground to sprout promotional seeds of your podcast. Let's delve into an elaborate guide on employing Facebook meticulously in your podcast promotional activities.

5.1. Building A Facebook Presence

First and foremost, you should establish your presence on Facebook. To materialize this, you should create either a Personal Profile (if you're promoting as an individual host) or a Business Page (if promoting as a brand or company). A well-optimized Facebook Page - adorned with a high-quality profile picture, a cover photo related to your podcast, and a concise, catchy description - is your first step towards initiating successful podcast promotion on Facebook.

5.2. Growing Your Facebook Community

Once you've claimed a digital corner on Facebook, your next objective should be to blossom a thriving community around your podcast. You can drive initial followers from your existing friends, family, and other networks. Inviting them to like, follow, and share your page is a good kickstart. Encourage listeners to like and follow your Facebook page, and therein participate in the discussions.

Through consistent communication, quality posts and proactive interactions, you can expand your Facebook community, further fueling your podcast's exposure.

5.3. Creating Engaging Content

It's essential to create content that depicts the character of your podcast and stirs interests among your target audience. Post updates about upcoming podcast episodes, snippets from previous episodes, behind-the-scenes content, and relevant informative or entertaining resources. Utilize Facebook's native tools like live video, polls, stories, and more. Engagement should be your top priority - craft your posts, whether photos, videos, links, or text, in such a way that it triggers likes, comments, shares, and discussions among your followers.

5.4. Leveraging Facebook Ads

Facebook Ads is a powerful tool to reach beyond your existing community. With the precision targeting options Facebook offers, you can reach potential listeners based on their demographics, interests, behaviors and more. For example, if your podcast centers around health and wellness, you can target users who have shown interest in related topics. You can run ad campaigns to promote your podcast, generate downloads, increase engagement on your posts or grow your page likes.

5.5. Utilizing Facebook Groups

Facebook Groups are an excellent avenue for finding and engaging with a community that shares interests with your podcast's genre. By actively participating in these groups, you can answer queries, provide valuable insights, and subtly reference your podcast. Creating your own Facebook Group with a focus on your podcast's primary theme can further drive engagement and listener loyalty.

5.6. Co-Promotion and Collaborations

Consider partnerships with other podcasters, influencers or relevant businesses for joint promotions. Sharing each other's content or organizing some 'live sessions' together can draw their audience to your podcast and vice versa. Co-promotion creates a win-win situation for both parties involved while amplifying your reach exponentially.

5.7. Analysing Facebook Metrics

Lastly, it's crucial to keep an eye on your Facebook metrics to gauge your strategy's effectiveness. Facebook's native insights tool offers a wealth of data like page likes, post reach, engagement, and more. Analyzing these indicators can help you discern what's working, what's not, and where you need to adjust your strategy. Remember, a successful Facebook strategy for podcast promotion is all about continual learning, experimentation, and adaptation.

We've now explored a comprehensive strategy for the effective promotion of your podcast on Facebook. Remember, consistency is key – remain active, engage with your community and keep delivering valuable, interesting content. Soon, you'll see how Facebook can be an incredible ally in your podcast's journey to success.

Chapter 6. Twitter: The Power of Tweets and Retweets

Without question, Twitter has emerged as one of the most influential social media platforms in the recent digital era. Its strength lies in its simplicity – short, sharp, and powerful messages that can have a global effect in the beat of a tweet. This chapter will dive deep into the heart of Twitter-centric strategies that could potentially be the catalyst for your podcast's growth.

6.1. Unleashing the Power of Tweets

We begin by comprehending the art of tweeting. A tweet's character limit might deter some from seeing its potential, but behind this brevity lies the true might of Twitter. A well-crafted tweet has the power to draw listeners to your podcast like bees to honey.

Your tweets should pursue to deliver one result: pique your audience's curiosity so they want to listen in. To accomplish this, craft content that elicits emotion, provokes thoughts, or teases value from your latest episode. For instance, if you've just interviewed an industry expert, share an intriguing quote from them. Forge tweets that are genuine, provide value, and resonate with your target audience.

It's also vital to use the right hashtags, especially those relevant to your podcast's genre or topic. This will expose your podcast to a broader audience who share an interest in your content themes. You can also engage with trending hashtags, but make sure they are congruent to your podcast's identity.

6.2. The Retweeting Phenomenon

Retweets serve as an essential engine for spreading your message. They occur when your followers share your tweet with their followers. This, in essence, is the heart of Twitter's potential virality. To amplify your retweet chances, create tweets with your audience's interests and preferences in mind. It invites them to share, letting your podcast gain wider visibility.

Scheduled posting during peak usage times is also beneficial. It helps you reach more people and increases the likelihood of further retweets. Services such as Tweriod or TweetDeck can help you identify these hours. Don't forget to include a call-to-action, cleverly urging followers to retweet - it drives up the numbers!

6.3. Under the Spotlight: Pinned Tweets

Pinned tweets are your personal marquees on Twitter. They remain at the top of your profile, offering users an immediate glimpse into your podcast's essence. Keep your latest, or most popular, episode here. Update it regularly in resonance with your publishing schedule. This serves as an automatic call-to-action to prospective listeners.

6.4. Direct Engagement: Reply, Like, Follow, and Repeat

Engagement on Twitter isn't solely about posting and retweeting; it requires interaction. Respond to comments left by followers to cultivate a community atmosphere. Liking tweets and following relevant users also boosts your visibility. Remember, Twitter is a social platform - your growth hinges on whether you're being "social" enough.

6.5. Turning Tweets into Listening Experiences with Twitter Audio Cards

For podcasters, Twitter Audio Cards are a pivotal tool. They enable users to listen to your podcast episode directly on Twitter without redirecting them to another app or webpage. It provides an immediate satisfying experience to listeners while keeping them on your Twitter feed.

6.6. Tracking Progress: Twitter Analytics

Ultimately, your Twitter strategy needs to be based on factual performance. Twitter's built-in analytics help you measure retweets, replies, likes, and the reach of your tweets. Frequent performance check-ins enable you to tweak your strategies based on what works best for your audience and your podcast.

To conclude, embracing Twitter's power involves bridging the gap between you and your listeners, transforming tweets into an amplified, echoed expressway of interactive content. Your followers aren't a mere growth statistic; they're your budding community and the voice that can help your podcast reverberate louder across the Twitterverse.

Chapter 7. Instagram: Boosting Your Podcast with Imagery

In a world where visuals speak louder than words, Instagram, a platform bustling with eye-catching images and engaging videos, provides an attractive avenue for taking your podcast to new heights. Exploiting the power of this visual medium can effectively augment your podcast's visibility, listenership, and overall engagement.

7.1. The Potency of Instagram in Podcast Promotion

Before delving into the nitty-gritty of Instagram strategies for podcast promotion, it is vital to understand the platform's inherent capacity to command attention. Instagram boasts over one billion active users each month, making it an invaluable tool for expanding your listener base. With its main demographic being ages 18-34, it provides an ideal staging ground for new ideas and fresh voices.

7.2. Establishing a Dedicated Account for Your Podcast

First and foremost, establish an Instagram account specifically dedicated to your podcast. This professional approach lets your listeners know they're in the right place and sets the stage for consistent brand imagery. It also allows more freedom when developing a content strategy exclusively centered on your podcast. The account handle should ideally bear the name of your podcast, making it easy for listeners to find and follow you.

7.3. Developing a Visually Arresting Instagram Aesthetic

Instagram, as a visually dominated platform, demands a focus on aesthetic. A consistent and compelling visual language tied into your podcast brand can build recognition and drive engagement. Select a cohesive color palette that aligns with your podcast's brand, tone, and vibe. Use this through your designs, typography, and photography for a consistent brand image.

7.4. Creating Content that Connects

Creating valuable, engaging, and visually captivating content is the core of Instagram. Your content can be a blend of podcast snippets, behind-the-scenes peeks, related quotes, guest highlights, listener testimonials, or other relevant posts that ignite interest and involvement. Canva, a user-friendly design tool, is a great place to start for creating stunning Instagram content.

7.5. Caption Crafting and Hashtags

Well-crafted captions play a leading role in inviting likes, comments, and shares. Strong, actionable language can encourage users to listen to your podcast, drop comments, or tag friends. Also, pinning a call-to-action at the top of your caption increases the likelihood of interaction. Implementing the strategic use of hashtags can also magnify your reach. These convey a message to Instagram's algorithm about your content's context and help your post surface in relevant user searches. Research and use hashtags relevant to your podcast's theme and audience.

7.6. Instagram Stories: A Casual Connect

Instagram Stories offer an informal, ephemeral touchpoint with your audience. They are a terrific channel to promote new episodes, request feedback, show behind-the-scenes glimpses, or conduct quick polls. You can create story highlight albums to keep this engaging content accessible beyond the usual 24 hour-story lifespan.

7.7. IGTV and Reels: The Video Vanguard

Instagram's feature-loaded extensions, IGTV and Reels, provide extended opportunities for content distribution. IGTV is perfect for longer form content where you can share full-length podcast episodes or interviews. Meanwhile, Reels, with its quick, snackable video content, can serve excellent teasers for new episodes. Both are powerful tactics for attracting and retaining listeners' attention.

7.8. Engage to Enlarge Audience

Finally, foster a sense of community through earnest engagement on Instagram. Respond proactively to comments, share shout-outs or user generated content, or conduct live Q&As to connect and converse with your listeners.

7.9. Leveraging Instagram Ads for Amplified Reach

A prime feature for businesses, Instagram Ads, can help boost your podcast's exposure. By defining your goals (brand awareness, reach, or engagement), and targeting the ads as per your desired listener demographics, you can enhance your podcast's visibility and potential listenership.

By harnessing Instagram's visually compelling and highly interactive capabilities, you can attract, engage, and grow your podcast audience like never before. Remember, the key to success on this platform, like all social media, lies not just in consistent posting but also in delivering value, building relationships, and staying authentic to your podcast's voice. Armed with these tips, you are ready to dive into the realm of Instagram and watch your podcast flourish!

Chapter 8. LinkedIn: Establishing Your Podcast in the Professional Network

Imagine stepping onto a platform where the audience is vast and diverse but chiefly designed for professionals who are keen on consuming worthwhile content. LinkedIn, the largest professional network, with its refined user base offers just that – an ideal platform to establish your podcast. This chapter will provide a detailed understanding and strategic plan to utilize LinkedIn for your podcast promotion. Unlike the more casual social media platforms like Instagram, Facebook, or Twitter, LinkedIn requires a unique approach due to its professional orientation and content type preference. Let's dive deep into the world of LinkedIn and explore how you can grow your podcast as a recognized professional network asset.

8.1. The Power of LinkedIn for Podcast Promotion

LinkedIn, with its professional climate, creates a unique environment that makes it perfect for promoting podcasts, particularly those that are business or industry-aligned. When it comes to content sharing, LinkedIn engenders an atmosphere of trust, credibility, and relevance that is unparalleled. Content that brings value or education, informative articles, thought leadership posts, industry specific insights - these elements work exceptionally well here, resonating with its user base and thereby potentially engaging a more receptive audience for your podcast. Furthermore, attributes like LinkedIn Learning platform and LinkedIn Groups provide a concentration of focused audience groups, adding another advantage to your podcast promotion strategy on this platform.

8.2. Creating a Winning LinkedIn Profile for Your Podcast

For effective podcast promotion, your LinkedIn profile needs to reflect your podcast's essence. Start by incorporating your podcast into the headline of your profile. This makes your podcast immediately noticeable to visitors. Use your profile's About section to give a rich, concise description of your podcast, along with the link leading directly to your podcast list. Remember, this area should articulate the value your podcast brings to the audience. Include keywords related to your podcast domain for better searchability. Use your Featured section to highlight your top podcasts, testimonials, or any upcoming episode teasers, and always keep it updated.

List.Template: * Podcast Name in Profile's Headline * Podcast Description in About Section * Podcast Link in About Section * Use Relevant Keywords * Highlight Key Podcasts or Related Content in Featured Section

8.3. Sharing Vibrant Podcast Content

LinkedIn provides ample opportunities for content sharing. Regularly share updates about new episodes, guests, topics, and behind-the-scenes footage. This generates curiosity and can lead to increased listenership. You can also create bite-sized video clips, infographics, or succinct write-ups from podcast conversations to tease and engage your audience. LinkedIn's professional audience appreciates such rich, informative content. Always craft your text copy invigoratingly to make your content more clickable and shareable.

List.Template: * Regular Updates about Podcast Episodes * Highlight

Key Speakers or Topics * Share Behind-the-scenes Footage * Create Bite-sized Clips, Infographics, Write-ups from Podcast * Engage Audience with Interesting Copy Text

8.4. Harnessing the Power of LinkedIn Pulse & Articles

Publishing long-form articles on LinkedIn Pulse enables you to showcase your podcast's insights further. Write articles recapping your episodes, or dive deeper into the topics discussed. Similarly, LinkedIn articles help foster thought leadership, increase your podcast's credibility, and often invite more in-depth audience engagement. Simultaneously, these articles serve as great supplementary content for your podcast, giving your audience a double dose of value.

8.5. Tapping into LinkedIn Groups & Learning Platform

LinkedIn Groups pool like-minded professionals and hence, could be a goldmine for finding your podcast's target audience. Engage, contribute, and share valuable content in relevant groups to create your network and attract listeners. To tap into the potential of LinkedIn Learning, consider creating a relevant course around your podcast topic. It's an excellent way to establish expertise, provide value to the community, and subtly promote your podcast.

8.6. Engaging with Followers and Encouraging Interaction

Just as on other social media platforms, engagement is key on LinkedIn. Respond to comments, participate in discussions, and appreciate your listeners' feedback. Also, don't forget to encourage your audience to share your posts, as it expands your podcast reach. Regular engagement will lead to a more robust network, increasing your podcast visibility and followership.

In conclusion, LinkedIn's unique professional landscape offers an untapped avenue for podcast promotion. It requires a slightly different approach yet can yield significant benefits if harnessed correctly. Here's to establishing your podcast in the professional network and leverage it for your podcast's phenomenal growth! Remember to be consistent, patient, and always willing to learn and adapt. The path to podcasting success on LinkedIn is paved with strategic and consistent actions!

Chapter 9. Cross-Promotion Strategies Across Social Platforms

In our relentless pursuit of better exposure, one key aspect playing an instrumental role is cross-promotion across social platforms. It opens up not just a realm of potential audiences, but whole galaxies. Let's delve deep into this topic, illuminating the strategies, revealing the nuances and shining a spotlight on the significant benefits of using cross-promotion strategies across platforms.

9.1. Establishing Pillars of Cross-Promotion

Successful cross-promotion across social platforms largely rests on four key pillars. These key components form the basis upon which subsequent strategies are built, and their mastery forms the cornerstones of successful initiatives.

1. **Synchronization:** Synchronization is the alignment of your messaging across various platforms. While the content you share on each platform might differ in nature, the core messaging should remain consistent. A unified and synchronized drive of information aids in reinforcing your brand message, making it resonate more powerfully with your target audience.

2. **Strategic Timing:** Delivering content to your audience at the right moment is crucial for maximum engagement. Leverage the various analytics tools offered by social platforms to understand your audience's activity trends. After you've derived these crucial insights, schedule your posts for those specific high engagement windows.

3. **Value Addition:** Ultimately, the content you share should enrich your audience in some way. Whether it's by offering entertainment, education, or empowerment, finding ways to add value to your audience's journey will encourage them to engage more with your content and stay loyal to your podcast.

4. **Engagement:** Value, when combined with engagement, leads to a robust and sustainable community. Leverage strategies that encourage your audience to participate in discussions, share your content, or even contribute to your podcast. Active participation fosters a sense of community, keeping audiences invested in your growth and success.

9.2. Mapping Social Platforms

Having understood the pillars of successful cross-promotion, our next step is to map the social platforms you'll be using, and understanding how each can be effectively utilized in your cross-promotion strategy. Here, we take a closer look at four major platforms - Facebook, Twitter, Instagram, and LinkedIn.

1. **Facebook:** With its massive, diverse user base, Facebook is a powerhouse for audience engagement. Create an active community by sharing behind-the-scenes stories, polls, and bringing them into your podcasting journey. Use Facebook Live for interactive Q&A sessions or teasers.

2. **Twitter:** Twitter shines with quick updates and interactions. Use this micro-blogging platform to share snippets, podcast highlights or quick tips. Regularly engage in trending discussions relevant to your podcast's subject matter.

3. **Instagram:** A platform heavily reliant on visual content, Instagram is perfect for showcasing graphics, charts, or behind-the-scenes photos. Use features like 'Instagram Stories' for sneak peeks, or 'IGTV' for extensive content related to your podcast.

4. **LinkedIn:** As a professional network, LinkedIn commands a

more serious and dedicated user base. This platform is excellent for sharing professional insights, thorough discussions or research related to your podcast topic.

9.3. Content Modulation Across Platforms

The art of cross-promotion is to modulate your content to align with the nature and preferences of the individual platforms. Here is how you can tailor your content across platforms:

1. **Same Message, Different Formats:** While the core message remains the same, consider the nature of the platform. Use images and videos for Instagram, succinct tweets for Twitter, long posts for Facebook, and professional insights or detailed posts for LinkedIn.

2. **Flex Your Creativity:** Use the diverse nature of these platforms to express your creativity. Unique graphics, innovative polls, captivating snippets, teaser trailers – the world is your canvas.

3. **Optimize for Platform's Algorithm:** Each platform has its own algorithm. Understand how it works, and tailor your content delivery strategy accordingly to maximize your reach and engagement.

9.4. Unleashing the Power of Cross-promotion

Having established sound strategies for cross-promotion, the path is now clear to implement these strategies and witness your podcast grow. A well-executed cross-promotion strategy is like a force multiplier, amplifying the reach of each individual platform, resulting in a much larger audience that's actively engaged and invested in your podcast. Multiply your questions, deliver multifold content, and earn exponential growth – make no mistake, this is the battlefield. Arm yourself with the right strategies and witness your podcast's phenomenal growth.

Remember, the key a successful cross-promotion strategy doesn't solely lie in reaching a large audience. It's also about engaging your audience, keeping them hooked over time, and fostering a collaborative community that supports and contributes to the growth of your podcast. So, strategically get your chess pieces into action, and let the game of cross-promotion elevate your podcast into an undisputed realm of success.

Chapter 10. Measuring Success: Metrics, Analytics, and Insights

To gauge and ensure the success of your podcast promotion, we turn to metrics, analytics, and insights on social media. Drawing from these three elements, you can measure your efforts' effectiveness, track your growth, and ultimately, reap the rewards of your promotional activities.

10.1. Understanding Podcast Metrics

Podcast metrics are critical to understanding your audience's size, behavior, and preferences. They help ascertain whether your promotional efforts are resonating with your audience or if they're falling on deaf ears.

The three primary podcast metrics are:

1. Downloads: This is one of the most commonly used metrics in podcasting. It's the analogue of 'page views' for websites. It measures how many times your podcast was downloaded, but it doesn't necessarily equate to listens.

2. Subscriptions: This metric shows how many listeners have subscribed to your podcast. A high subscription rate means your content resonates with your listeners and they're eager for more episodes.

3. Listener Retention: This metric gauges how long your audience listens to each episode. If your listeners tend to drop off after a few minutes, this might indicate that your content isn't engaging or that your episodes are too lengthy.

In addition to these, you should also pay attention to listener reviews and ratings, as they provide qualitative feedback and give you insights into your audience's sentiments.

10.2. Leveraging Social Media Analytics

While podcast metrics give you insights into your podcast's performance, social media analytics help you understand the effectiveness of your promotional efforts. Understanding social media-related metrics will empower you to adjust your promotion strategies accordingly.

Here are some of the key social media analytics to study:

1. Reach: This metric refers to the total number of unique users who viewed your content.

2. Impressions: This metric reflects the total number of times your content was displayed, irrespective of clicks or engagement.

3. Engagement: This metric measures the total interactions on your content, including likes, shares, comments, and other reactions.

4. Followers Growth: This metric shows the change in your followers count over a specific time frame, providing a clear picture of your audience growth.

5. Click-Through Rate (CTR): This measures the percentage of your audience that clicks on the link in your post to your podcast.

10.3. Harnessing Insights

Insights combine data from both podcast metrics and social media analytics to provide actionable strategies for your podcast promotion. These insights allow you to take what you've learned and apply it to enhance your promotional efforts and increase your podcast's reach, engagement, and audience growth.

Some of the key insights you might gain from your data include:

1. Optimal Posting Times: By analyzing when your audience engages with your content the most, you can schedule your posts at these times to maximize their reach and engagement.

2. Content Preferences: By looking at engagement rates on different types of posts, you can figure out what sort of content resonates with your audience the most.

3. Audience Demographics: Understanding who your audience is can inform your content creation and promotion strategies.

10.4. Using Analytics Tools

Using comprehensive analytics platforms can automate the data gathering and analysis process, making it easier to track and compare your metrics. Some popular choices include Google Analytics, Sprout Social, Buffer, and Buzzsprout. These tools provide in-depth reports and insights that can help you streamline your podcast promotion process.

In conclusion, understanding how to navigate and harness metrics, analytics, and insights is critical for measuring your tactical efforts' success and refining your strategies over time. It allows you to identify areas of improvement, optimize your promotional strategies, and stay on the path to podcast prosperity. This chapter should have equipped you with the necessary awareness to leverage these vital tools. Therefore, it's time you tuned into the data and let it guide your podcast to resounding success on social media!

Chapter 11. Case Studies: Successful Podcast Promotion Using Social Media

The exploration of case studies serves as a dynamic approach to unearth real-world success stories, practical lessons, and fruitful strategies that have paved the way for remarkable triumphs in podcast promotion with social media. This chapter unveils diverse stories of podcasts that have capitalized on social media platforms for amplified reach and sublime growth. With each story, you'll find a unique take on social media strategies that you can mould and incorporate into your podcast promotion journey.

11.1. Story of 'The Daily'

'The Daily', a presentation from The New York Times, is a stellar example in mastering the art of podcast promotion on social media. Garnering millions of listeners worldwide, 'The Daily' has harnessed the power of platforms such as Twitter and Facebook to engage its audience and keep the momentum of exponential podcast growth.

One of the most effective strategies 'The Daily' employs involves exploiting the interactive nature of social media. The team regularly posts episodic highlights or thought-provoking questions that ignite engaging conversations among listeners, forming a tightly-knit online community.

Besides, Twitter threads featuring snippets or salient points from an episode have been a potent tool for 'The Daily'. This tactic not only provides substantial content to followers who might have missed an episode but also re-engages those who have listened, inviting them to contribute to the conversation.

11.2. Success with Social Media: 'Call Your Girlfriend'

Next, we turn our attention towards the quintessentially millennial podcast, 'Call Your Girlfriend'. This podcast has brilliantly capitalized on Instagram's visually led platform to etch a solid presence. Twice a week, the podcast leverages the Instagram Stories feature to share tidbits from their most recent episode.

They also cleverly utilize the 'Swipe Up' feature, providing followers direct access to the episode. What's more, the team behind 'Call Your Girlfriend' doesn't shy away from putting their faces front and center on social media – a personalized and authentic touch that strengthens their bond with their audience.

11.3. 'Science Vs' and Facebook Promotion

This case presents how 'Science Vs', a podcast from Gimlet Media, used Facebook to extend its reach and witness phenomenal growth. Through regular and engaging posts, from episode snippets to behind-the-scenes shots, the podcast manages to pique listener interest and boost engagement.

What stands out about 'Science Vs' is their clever use of Facebook Groups. They have formed a community for listeners, where they promote their new broadcasts, initiate discussions, and answer listener questions. This interaction has led to increased audience engagement and transformed listeners into avid promoters of the podcast.

11.4. LinkedIn Mastery: 'The Ed Mylett Show'

'The Ed Mylett Show' stands as a shining example of effectively utilizing LinkedIn for podcast promotion. Through key strategic moves such as sharing podcasts with thought-provoking write-ups, attaching relevant hashtags, and encouraging sharing among followers, the host Ed Mylett ensured his show resonated with professionals on LinkedIn.

One distinguishing feature of this promotion strategy lies in presenting each episode's content as an opportunity for professional growth. This narrative significantly appeals to the LinkedIn audience, accelerating the podcast's reach and popularity.

These case studies offer valuable insights into the practical application of social media strategies for podcast promotion. While every podcast is unique in its style and audience, these strategies provide a basis for creating promotion campaigns that resonate with the desired audience and amplify the podcast's reach across the social media realm. Remember that success in social media promotion is not achieved overnight but is a testament to consistent efforts, strategic planning, and iterative learning from analyses and feedback. These stories of success should serve as an inspiration and a blueprint, but your unique podcast promotion journey should be tailored to align with your target listeners' tastes and expectations.